The Invisible Kings

DAVID MORLEY was born in Blackpool and is of partly Romani descent. A natural scientist by background, he has published eight collections of poetry, and his work has won many writing awards, including the Arts Council Raymond Williams Prize, a Hawthornden International Writers Fellowship and an Eric Gregory Award. He also writes essays, criticism and reviews for *The Guardian* and *Poetry Review*. He directs the Warwick Writing Programme at the University of Warwick where he is a professor and winner of a National Teaching Fellowship. He is the author of *The Cambridge Introduction to Creative Writing*.

T0159861

Also by David Morley

POETRY
Releasing Stone
A Belfast Kiss
Mandelstam Variations
Clearing a Name
A Static Ballroom
Scientific Papers
Ludus Coventriae

NON-FICTION
Under the Rainbow: Writers and Artists in Schools
The Cambridge Introduction to Creative Writing

AS EDITOR/CO-EDITOR
Northern Stories 2 (with Philip Callow and Maura Dooley)
The New Poetry (with Michael Hulse and David Kennedy)
Of Science (with Andy Brown)
The Gift
Phoenix New Writing
No Longer Poetry: New Romanian Poets (with Leonard Aldea)
Collected Poems of Geoffrey Holloway

FILM
Gujarat Grand Mushairas

DAVID MORLEY

The Invisible Kings

CARCANET

First published in Great Britain in 2007 by
Carcanet Press Limited
Alliance House
Cross Street
Manchester M2 7AQ

A CIP catalogue record for this book is available from the British Library
ISBN 978 1 85754 905 8

The publisher acknowledges financial assistance from Arts Council England

Typeset by XL Publishing Services, Tiverton
Printed and bound in England by SRP Ltd, Exeter

for the Invisible Kings or for the Bears

Acknowledgements

To the editors of the following publications where all these poems, or versions of them, were first published: *Avocado*, *Babylon Burning* (Nth Position), *Leviathan Quarterly*, *The Liberal*, *The London Magazine*, *The London Review of Books*, *New Writing 12* (edited by Jane Rogers, Blake Morrison and Diran Adebayo; Picador), *New Writing 14* (edited by Lavinia Greenlaw and Helon Habila; Granta), *One Hundred Poets Against the War* (edited by Todd Swift; Salt Publications), *Orbis Litterarum*, *Poetaster*, *Poetry Review*, *PN Review*, *Quadrant* (Australia), *The Poets Letter*, *The Rialto*, *Stand*, *Warp and Weft* (The Worple Press).

'Ludus Coventriae' was commissioned by the Coventry Phoenix Project and Vivian Lovell of the Public Arts Commissioning Agency. Peter Larkin first published a full version alongside other poems in a chapbook of that name (Prest Roots). A sculptural version of part of this poem, 'Processional', is engraved in bronze 60 metres long by 0.35 metres, on permanent display in the Garden of International Friendship in Coventry. Peter Mack, Siobhan Keenan and Christiania Whitehead gave scholarly help as I wrote the first version of 'Ludus Coventriae'. Many thanks to Roy Fisher for permission to use three lines from 'The Entertainment of War' as the epigraph to 'Ludus Coventriae'.

This volume's epigraph is the final line of *The Excursion to the Forest* from Czesław Miłosz's sequence 'The World'. *The Invisible Kings* is the second section of a cycle that began with *Scientific Papers* (Carcanet). An early version of *The Invisible Kings* was looked at in manuscript by Siobhan Keenan, as well as by the Peters B, C, D: Blegvad, Carpenter and Davidson, and Zoë Brigley and Andy Brown.

Poscia non sia di qua vostra reddita
Purgatorio I

Contents

A Readers' Guide or Patrìn

Romani words are given in English translation at the foot of the page. The alphabet used in the language here is phonetic. Each sound is represented by its own letter or letter combination. The words are pronounced exactly as they appear.

You Were Broken

for Les Murray

The amazed, massing shade
for the glacial valley, made
from a single araucaria
that smashed its way
by micrometers of birth-push
under five centuries of dusks
of carbon dioxide and rainfall,
while the volcanic rocks made landfall
against its unrolled, harbouring roots;

and the roots took the rocks in their arms
and placed them, magically,
like stone children, about itself
as it unfolded its fabulous tale:
of the wood heart mourned to flint
by slow labour and loneliness,
by what it could not reach, yet see
at distance, and of the sound of that sea,
and of the cruel brightness

of butterflies and grasses,
foreknowledge of their brevity,
of a heard stream, overhearing
prints of otters on its plane stones,
gold wagtails sprying over
the gravel and shallows of courtship;
of orange blames of gall-wasps, honey fungus,
the watch-turning of tree-creepers;
of blights of summer lightning,

of fire damage and that dark
year's mark worn secretly,
a ring, forged inside a ring;
then the winter's coronation closing
in a swaying crown of redwings,
cones, drab diagonals of pine-fall,
the lead winds hardening, and while
the stone children wept with rain
the great tree sheltered them.

In Cold Dimensions

I study the lives on a leaf: the little sleepers, numb nudgers in cold dimensions

A strange way to see.
   A stranger's way.
Her garden is an exhibition
   with lit rooms, masterpieces,
and her rooms are parterres;
   the shape and size of their levels
calculated to the soil-grain,
   the spaces between shadowed
gnomons; those data-breaks
   called seasons hold
hallmarks and prints:
   temperature's drafting.

She explains that there are masters
   as there are spadesmen,
that both are speculators;
   that the gruff grafters
who break soil, sieve weed,
   are the salts of creation. Yet
that is not the actual work –
   this arises by intangible
skill, by flaw, flawed
   experiment even, and her own
interventions. The stranger:
   she must always be welcomed.

These then are her gardens.
    Her four-shadowed sundial.
Scent of snow on the breeze.
    Sun pawing on your shoulders.
Ripe buds quelling colour
    before they broadcast leaf
as if to foreshadow winter.
    A strange, constant season.
The moon sails in a wrack
    of steady cirrus and sleet.
On the lip of that world
    she turns to take your hand.

Now, from her black soil,
    storytellers and artists
begin to erupt: cramoisy
    abstracts from peony and poppy,
dripped inks of algae
    igniting on a dew-pond;
butterfly narratives
    of flight, where they settle
to sip, unfold wings
    on illuminated parchment
on a comparison of palettes,
    on the wherewithal of pattern.

There, come her rich fables
    in which lacewings balance
against ground-level winds:
    the viewless khamsins,
zephyrs and harmattans,
    that sway towers of digitalis;
and in the foxglove mouths
    humble-bees move
edgily at their easels;
    dragonflies, hummingbirds
freeze and spurt above oils,
    histrionic, in counter-worlds.

Now are her apprentices
   to works in progress:
under the pearl pond's surface
   bent brushes of fly larvae
on canvas below a lily's pad:
   two poles of a planet –
one in loom, one in radiance –
   half-conceiving of the other;
a toad hunkers over them,
   a levitating Brahma,
lax tutor of the green school
   of watercolour, of water.

Here, her miniatures move
   into sight: the eye delves
hinterlands where the unmanaged
   survive under a slew of brick
lobbed by the first gardener.
   Lever the frore mortar
to parallel cities of red ants,
   woodlice, gaunt generations
of black frost and feelers,
   unnoticed deaths, languages,
births, ice architecture.
   Their great roof falls back.

At length, among the etching
   blades of spear and couch
grass, the factions of colour
   freeze to clear light.
A solitary, strange season.
   In her lit outline
the garden shows a wall,
   then a gate to the space
where she will let you
   stand apart from yourself.
At the lip of the world.
   She releases your hand.

Paul Celan: Draft of a Landscape

Light grows from the ground, from basalt seeds,
from laval hardwiring. At the heart of the earth
a stone saddle, the blazing brows of animals.
The wells of our graves are in place. The steps
to them cleansed of their wreckage, of their blood.

Of the Genus Diatomaceae

The sea's rooms darken.
  Wanting myself dead we watch
  from the boat as the billion
  iridescent diatoms make
  their fleering climb towards night
  from the steep of the depths:
  that dark, swarming fleet,
  every porthole eyed with flame,
  lighting now at the form
of a mirrored and a total moon.

Patrìn

for Jacqueline Morley

or *pateran,*
pyaytrin, or *sikaimasko.*
The marker used by Roma
that tells others of their direction,
often grids of branches or leaf-twists or
bark-binds. Used for passing on news
using prearranged forms, patterns
or permutations of these. Yet
it also means a leaf or,
simply, a page.

Simply, a page
yet it also means a leaf
or permutations of these
using prearranged forms, patterns.
Bark-binds used for passing on news,
often grids of branches or leaf-twists
that tell others of their direction.
The marker used by Roma:
pyaytrin, or *sikaimasko,*
or *pateran.*

Sikavnò

The lathe
we were at
kept cutting out
in little deaths.
Our anger slid.
Under a blade
sheet-metal split.
I stood where
my father stood me:
this side of a lathe.
Weathers of dust
fell to a hush
at his feet.

I did
what he asked:
watched callipers twitch
legs skinny, an avocet's;
but looked beyond
to drill-heads, primed,
fluted like wands of steel.
He halved the work:
held mandrels, clamp.
Drill-heads spoke
for him, talked
themselves out.

sikavnò: a teacher

Icicle-steel

Two
lines
scribed
on steel –
my father's
poetry;
all I read
is swarf
spooling
off blades –
icicle-steel –
ghost-chatter
of lathes;
not this,
this cutting
the metal
of speech,
commas like
weld-scars;
his life work
with steel:
acetylene
a plume
an icicle.

Finn of the Wiles

The Finn was lolling over some nicked bike,
or a poor rich kid's skinny moped,
giving everyone the crim stare, the come-on.
There was his mother for you –
The Blackpool Tower in fox fur –
supped husbands by the pint, kept a round of them on tab,
then took a shine to the next wallet down the bar.
Not anybody's fault, mind. They're a bad influence, those Finns.
Nick them, book them, chuck the bloody book at them
– they're back, bad as pennies.
I tell you something for nothing, those pennies
roll home from wherever they've been slotted.
'I have changed my life, your Honour.'
For the interim. *Changed your locks, have you?*

I'd be at my comp, but The Finn,
he chose a brighter school:
the penny arcades on Blackpool Prom,
spent the day chancing bets
– those toy racehorses jerking to a photo finish.
He'd lurk at the school gates
with a face on to show off his thievings.
Allen keys. Bike gears.
A tin snooker trophy.
Small spuds and small beer no burglar bothers with,
but first prizes for The Finn.
He got banged up for something bigger.
The Finn surfaced paler, stranger,
behind the fish-skin wheel of a Cortina.

It was something to do with my brother
and the back hand of some police bother.
I cursed The Finn to his face, spat his name on his shoes,
but The Finn, he didn't lift a finger.
Later, he was lights out on a cell floor.
The coppers let him ride out his asthma.
By the evening, he was old.

At dawn, they found him cold.
Runt Finn, they said, you're running nowhere.
Finn of the Wiles. Finn of the Filch, with his pickers and stealers.
I saw him out of depth a hare in the open,
antennal ears, rickety lope,
dodging the police on the Golden Mile.
In a swirl of litter, something or, nothing the shape of him.

Fiction

I was haunted by falsehood from the start, some brink of this reached
by late childhood. To keep lying, to pile it up, was how to live
because fiction tied the parts and parcels of name. Fiction was the poached
life history of travelling folk. Fiction was the electricity and rates.
Paid for your shoes. Fiction took the bus to the store, was allowed
by family law to shoplift. Fiction told the old story every night.
Fiction was poor but dishonest. Fiction gave birth before a grate,
placed my placenta on the sizzling clinkers. Fiction liked comforts.
She had the brains to earn them, but Fiction stayed out late.
Fiction was a virgin before marriage, of course. She laid the hoard
of the tale tall before you. You were bidden to believe in this
despite the fact it was fiction. You had to grow askew. It's hard
quarrelling with Fiction. Because Fiction is you: your bones
are thin beams of fable; and your blood, when it pouts at your lips
draws through its black alley. Fiction has good fingers, she has sewn
then unstitched the same shroud for years. Fiction longs for reunion
with her lover. He died strong and striking. He swam out of turn
down a long and burning sea of blood. Fiction yearned to restring the yarn
for herself, demanded a better ending. Her children learned their part
and played it from affection. But Fiction began to believe her tale.
                    It collapsed into art
in which Fiction was the lead, and her children chapters and verses.
Her friends would spin about her screaming *Author, Author.*
Haunted by so much falsehood, a brink was reached.

Widowed, one-breasted, Penny's world had shrunk to Blackpool.
Seventh child of seventh child, she could count on so, so little
except second sight, closed her curtains as though for a passing hearse,
dealt her tarot cards at neighbours, and sat there, weather-wise.
Picture how a claw hammer angles under a settled nail,
grinds against the top grain, then slides out the clean metal
fresh from first hammering. Penny works her audience,
and with her claw for grief, she plies her darkened séance.
An unknown sound is ground for a gnomic reading.
Ghosts arrive on time. Her sister's upstairs frapping
the floor: one tap for 'no', twice for 'yes', with three
slow *bumps* for some spiritualistic ambiguity.
Her son hangs about the back, wanting to beat their lights out,
break wide the curtains, reverse the sham night,
drive out the wake of widowers preening in their desire,
mouthing their childish pleas for another wife and mother.
For Penny in fact. She squats in her power, plays gypsy,
terraces a track the family goes up from loyalty to lie:
home as vardo, road as drom, life as one big bengipè.
Her suitors simper. They nose their dregs of tea.
Levering against one man's memories, Penny overhears the singing
of his dead wife. It's as if Penny were leaning against air, listening;
as if she were finding the proper angles for that slip soul
fresh from its first making. She drags out the clean metal.

vardo: a Gypsy's cart or caravan; **drom**: a road; **bengipè**: a trick or a quirk

Sèsi o Lety U Písku

I have come a long way and am almost there.
'You were almost there except for this frontier.'
I approach the frontier and see the wire.
'You passed me without looking but I was still present.'
I am almost there except for this frontier.
'There was nothing to stop you yet you rode back to the city.'
You pass me without looking but I am still present.
'Except for the wire there was nothing to stop you.'
There is nothing to stop me yet I ride back to the city.
'You made the brass boast you stopped for one night.'
Except for the wire there is nothing to stop me.
'And you saw this wire. It made you exceptional.'
I make the brass boast I'll stop there one night.
'It made you exceptional. Apart from the others.'
I see that wire. It makes me exceptional.
'Apart from the others, who stared back through the wire.'
It makes me exceptional: apart from the others.
'And you approached the frontier. And saw the wire.'
A part of the others. They stare back through the wire:
You came a long way. You are almost there.

sèsi: a voice; **Lety U Písku**: the site of a concentration camp for Roma from Bohemia

A Rainbow

The caravans' windows run with pre-rainbow light, that skyline twisting
to twine where the women of the gypsy camp sling their yellow washing.
Target-practice, they reckon, *for the village men, come the drinking hours.*
Washtubs, tail-chasing mutts, tail-spin car wrecks...The small change
of children spills from the indigo of shrubs, faces in the uplight violet
from their dad's roadside forges. Late, they run for the tin school-bus.
From the buds of their blowtorches, those fathers work written-off, rotten steel
until it's blue, hammerable – rattleable as a thunder-box – then slam it, red,

into green
washing sluice, their children leaping through the steam as if they grew from it.

Te Avel Angle Tute

Sabàlen

A sloped road, red winter, every thorn lancet.
Ice riming each bared branch;
thrushes thaw in their doze
as light ripens over
alarms of berries
in their vermilion despite.
Thrush-song, welling in the ear
of that higher song-thrush, as alert, on its tree tower.

Chakmàkoos

Verglas shrugged from a caravan's glacial oilcloth.
Three travellers wake under the dead
load of a shared blanket;
stars still visible
and the blink of planets.
They yawn steam; three rising
breaths from the black tea slopped in iron
cans, fierce and numb, against those hardened hands.

Pàttrimìshi

Outside, a lapwing swells his wingspan
so it smacks on the air
one dozen times
a second
setting up
a drumming that fros
and falls in lap after lap as
the bird rounds and re-bounds
off the earth in his drift and mastery.

Tsiknyà

After the clattered wood steps are locked
the three travellers set to : to
order stone to stone
in a circle on
the turf hard
by a hedge's lea.
Two crack twigs, carve flames in palms;
the third christens the fire thickly with Four Star.

te avel angle tute: may this be before you; sabàlen: at daybreak; chakmàkoos: flint and iron;
pàttrimìshi: a legend; tsiknyà: a smell of burning

Shookàr Mooklò Chàv

'The Bonnie Broukit Bairn'

Mars is lacshòo in har lalò,
Venus in charyalò kesh diklò,
O poorò Moon khelèl sovnalò peri,
Their starry horatibà chalalìparipè,
Sparin' khanchik, na dyooshyoondinè
Earth, dàle shookàr mooklò chàv!
— *But ruv an' in àsoos you'll drown*
O sastò àshariba!

After Hugh MacDiarmid

shookar: beautiful; **mooklò**: abandoned; **chàv**: child; **lacshòo**: fair, handsome; **har lalò**: crimson, deep and red; **charyalò**: green; **kesh**: silk; **diklò**: Romani shawl; **o poorò**: the old; **khelèl**: shake (v); **sovnalò**: golden (adj); **peri**: feathers; **horatibà**: talk; **chalalìparipè**: load of nonsense [chalalì: foolishness, paripè: load (n)]; **khanchik**: nothing; **na dyooshyoondinè**: no thought; **dàle**: you dear! (voc); **ruv**: weep; **àsoos**: tears; **o sastò àshariba**: the whole wrestling match. Please see the original poem in the notes at the close of this book.

I am black, but comely, O ye daughters of Jerusalem, as the katòoni of Kedar, as the perdès of Solomon.

I have compared thee, O mi dèhiba, to chatimè gras in Pharaoh's vardos.

For while the king beshàv at his sharibè, my spikenard sendeth forth the soong thereof.

Behold, thou art lacshòo, mi dèhiba; behold, thou art lacshòo, thou hast goorgoorìtsa yakh.

For I am the rose of Sharon, and the parnò looloodì of the har.

As the parnò looloodì among karòs, so is mi dèhiba among her cshays.

Stay me with flagons, comfort me with aphai: for I am nasvalòo of kamav.

For I charge you, o ye cshays of Jerusalem, by the surnà, and by the surnà of the oomalyàkom, that ye stir not up, nor awake mi dèhiba, till mangàva.

Looloodì appear on the doonyàs, the tsìros of chiriklògìlyaiba is come, and the sèsi of the goorgoorìtsa is heard in our phoov.

Take us to the weshjooks, the tsikooroo weshjooks, that spoil the vitsa: for amarò vitsa have parus drakhà.

Until sabàlen, and the oochipè flees away, ìrin, mi dèhiba, and be thou like a roe or a ternò surnà upon the plàyna of Bether.

I will rise now, and go about the fòros in the òolitsa, and in the boohlò putèka I will seek him, my ozì piryamlòo: I sought him, amà I found him not.

Avàv from Lebanon, my rom, avàv from Lebanon: dikhav from the hip of Amana, from the hip of Shenir and Hermon, from the dens of aslàni, from the plàyna of leopards.

Ko adavkhà that cometh out of the wilderness like pillars of thoov, smelling of myrrh and frankincense, with all powders of the Roma?

Spikenard and saffron; calamus and cinnamon, with all trees of frankincense; myrrh and aloes, with sòvra spices.

For King Solomon has made himself a vardo of the kash of Lebanon.

katòoni: tents; perdès: curtain; mi dèhiba: my love, my beloved; chatimè gras: a company of horse assembled; Pharaoh or Firaòni: the Gypsy King of the Gypsy fairy tales or 'paramisi'; vardos: wagons; beshàv: sits; sharibè: table; soong: smell; lacshòo: fair, handsome; goorgoorìtsa yakh: dove's eyes; parnò looloodì: white flower [lily]; har: valley; karòs: thorns, stings (n); cshays: daughters; aphai: apples; nasvalòo: sick; kamav: love; surnà: deer; oomalyàkom: field; mangàva: wishes, pleases

looloodì: flowers; doonyàs: earth; tsìros: time; chiriklògìlyaiba: singing of birds; sèsi: voice; goorgoorìtsa: dove; phoov: land; weshjooks: foxes; tsikooroo weshjooks: little foxes; vitsa: vine; amarò: our; parus: soft; drakhà: grapes; sabàlen: daybreak; oochipè: shadow; ìrin: turn around; ternò surnà: young deer; plàyna: mountain; fòros: city; òolitsa: streets; boohlò: broad; putèka: paths; ozì piryamlòo: soul's lover; amà: but; avàv: come (imp); rom: husband, spouse; dikhav: look; hip: top; aslàni: lions; ko adavkhà: who is this; thoov: smoke; Roma: Gypsy [travelling merchant]; sòvra: all; vardo: wagon; kash: wood

The Gypsy Kings

Red wagons brush nettle towers,
smoking with pollen.

Sun drives off the dew.
The world steams, shakes with us.

Kings

for Siobhan Keenan

This here, brothers, sisters, is the title of a book, the head-work of an old king
of Romani land: the Tribunal, or the dispute between
the wise man and the world; or the death-sentence
passed by the soul upon the body.

from the *Book of the Wisdom of the Egyptians*

Introduction

This poem tells the journeys and trials of a wise fool, a Romani man maybe more used to the twin worlds of Roma and Gajo than he will freely allow. He is a fellow-traveller of the blacksmiths' tribe, the Boorgoodjìdes, useful to them for his part as their shaman.

The poem is a fairytale, once upon a time. The scenes are set in no country but in many countries the borders of which are invisible. The time frames coincide with certain events in Eastern Europe, but the persecution of Roma has been permanent and is a story that lies outside written histories. Yet the poem is also the man's history as he remembers it, and sings it.

ঽ

In this poem, the Romani language offers an opening, not a fence, between fields of language. Romani contains so many words and phrases from other languages; language is absorbed as it is travelled through. The words are pronounced exactly as they appear, and their meaning is best caught by reading the story at a canter, and without leaning too hard into the glossary. When a Romani word has two or more meanings in English, all those meanings are in play.

24

I

1933

I beg of you believe in the Kings, the blacksmiths' tribe, the Boorgoodjìdes
made up of the tamar, true twisters of sàstra, sras or srastrakàni,

who jam the jagged srast in the jaws, the chamàhoolya,
of their kerpèdy, and ply it, plume it polokès then plakomè

that way and this, rotating it like wire, until it's rinimè, roopoovalò,
arced into white rings, into angroostì, necklaces, into the bright akanootnò.

I am the kings' man, asanòo mànoosh, all smiles, ahmàtsi manoosh…
the kings' fool gadaveskè I bear you belief, forge you four words, shtar hòrata:

four stars to follow: patyàv, apakyàv, patsyàva, or apatyàv. You must pick
or be picked; be picked up or picked off. Like kopanàri, the carver

one choice to your chisel, one sting to your karò, one karò to our thorn.
Asanòo mànoosh, 'all smiles', I can wait for you but, tooryalìste, I circle you.

I am circling you. In the court of the hayfields I am circling you;
in the laws of the hedgerows I run on the field-side, oomalyàkom,

you keeping the drom: I invisible, audible, a flume of finches blowing
through the thornfields at your riding. This conduct I keep for my kings:

heralding them at the sharp cities, their seer, speaker. Tall at fòros-gates
I cry, both falsely and truly: 'Mande will sollohaul neither bango nor tatcho!

Hold the holtà of patsyàva, it should surround you like oopràlyavinate,
be more than a night-belief, a rakyàsapatyàv, or needless nightmare.

Boorgoodjìdes sleep sound in their double-world, graft even in dreams, barely
bezèti,
for what's righteous in speech, chachoonò, is word-twin for what's real

like their right-wrought srastrakàni, so it is byword with their cshib, their chachès…
Now – I bring you, Gajo, to be bridvà, rokker with us, and to deal!'

Night-hosted beneath city walls, our tent posts forestial,
salchinyalò; our hounds hang tense against tying poles,

a hundred hungers of them not counting the tsikooroo zhookels
woofing white clouds as the snow, harèef's heft, lulls against tentflaps.

I slide out to find rum, snow snaring my bootòoshi,
draggling my gait drunk. Guards on the stràha cat-call and caper,

bowl snowballs from high; bury coins in their white breasts.
One soldier holds up a tahtùy of vodka, tries to toss it, gives up trying,

tips the matòo neat on a snowball, doughs it hand to hand
then hurls the hard drink down to me. Kibir kurla? I joke and, Hoolanò!

as I play up the tsirkajìs, half-practising for our tsìrka,
clowning beneath the storm clouds of coin-snow and snow-vodka.

Agor of their watch I have snowballs, but no command,
my tongues are twigs for basket weaving, choochoonya, rayà,

but my jèpa's jammed with ice-hatalì, jingling as I slither
polokès to the tents, kurpìzavà my kaltsa. You have seen me

as I am, dooymooyalò Gajo, dead-legged and dyàslis iphoo,
out cold on my bed with the dark dogs about me. I am summoned,

sovavnò, for bùlnoozyava. The drink holds open doors to my dream,
a lamàda of memory on which the kings scribe their raroriò razprèyzila.

Ahmàtsi manoosh, but this is my mastery. This night I am ready.
I rokker their story back, circling them, track my tale into the gerdèy,

riding the rare roads, until I sleep hòratiba, dream-speaking their romanipè,
speaking it plain as I have heard it. Just as I spell this spell: *delpesgodì* ——

Kings bend about my bed, eavesdrop on my night-speech. Trills and lulls,
owlcalls and answerings. The tentpoles wrestling above our canopies

grow woodland in my mind. One blacksmith pours wine, softly; it suggests
a strayed stream within me, plying under tree canopies, koonjoopàte, where it will.

The kings cock their ears for speech of their own species. They hear nothing
but my wood-mimicry: retchka and retchko, ràrtigìllichal, a rùkkersamèngri
                                                                                                  churring,

kackaràtchi and kàulochìrilo, a weshjook sniffing wiffler, bìttikànni, bàrripòari...
I am the kings' seer, their bestiary. I am old now; I have many voices in me.

They are patient; they have ridden longer distances than my memory,
know I must sing the earth over before I find my sèsi. I burn on this bed.

They lift my lapsed palms, chafe them between locked hands,
douse the embers of my eyes with eef, with the skins of iced erikin.

When my arms ignite above me, my watchers sponge them over
as if my limbs were lit swords being doused in their making.

Cease snow.   Stream shadow.   Owl now to the owl's hole.
Through the thicket of wood-speech, wildbirds back to their branches:

oopràlyavinate, my chosen hour. It is dawn when my voice breaks:
'There will be a fair in that fòros, races and trading, our stallions steaming

in their stamped paddocks. You will go in the gate with the morning.
Fear nothing save the price of town-charcoal. Fear everything

save the pride of your màstooroos. Leave me now. But leave town by evening.
There is something behind, false water at distance. Prosper, but wear warning.

Where the river rises beyond their stone-ford, a deeper ford is laden
with piled lèshi, shoodrò, some of them limb-slight. I see the faces of children.'

Sabàlen. The kings are gone. I make my way to the len.
Seven silver shire horses wade, their tails whishing ice-shell in its shallows,

grandfathers in their gravitas. I kick out a wash-pool, yakh of panyalò,
a small eye of water, in which to salve my soldered eyes. An ice-quake

of verglas, a chain of little gunshots; the horses crunch backwards,
backing on to the bryàgoos. There is nobody coming, or watching.

I shave into the moving mirrors of underriver. Randlò, I untether
my light body from its hides and wools, from the skins of surnà,

lathe myself over; let the heat of my dream dry myself before
the cold engulfs me. Only then do I see the kookoochìn aiming

their green darts through the cloths of evènd, the cloths of pàhni,
heads hanging like the erlìdes ashamed of their earliness,

their eagerness to settle. I will not pick these. I will not pick her.
A woman steps over the riverbank, parusyoov melts beneath her

revealing the garavdò, the veiled and unsmelted. I will not remember.
Even as she stands, the light thaw quickens. The horses hove to,

graze at her feet, untethered, knowing her whisper, her weather.
I know only winter, and the tamar, true twisters of the sàstra.

Theirs is my ring now, my field, my bright akanootnò.
But I am not of the tribe. I have neither fathers nor mothers.

I stand outside the town walls with horses and flowers.
I am 'the back one', 'the one behind', the good paloonò,

their teller of futures, rarorikanès, their dreams' traveller.
I watch her ghost kneel among the snowdrop beds by the river.

Boorgoodjìdes: the blacksmiths' tribe; **tamar**: ironsmiths; **sàstra, sras, srastrakàni, srast**: iron (n); **chamàhoolya**: jaws (n, pl); **kerpèdy**: pliers; **polokès**: slow (adv); **plakomè**: squashed, pressed (adj); **rinimè**: filed (adj); **roopoovalò**: silver (adj); **angroostì**: rings (n); **akanootnò**: the present, the contemporary (n); **asanòo mànoosh**: a smiling man; **ahmàtsi manoosh**: a foolish man; **gadaveskè**: because; **shtar hòrata**: four words; **patyàv, apakyàv, patsyàva**, or **apatyàv**: belief (n); **kopanàri**: woodcarver; **karò**: means both thorn (n) and sting (n); **tooryalìste**: circling movement or manoeuvre; **oomalyàkom**: field; **drom**: road; **fòros**: city [or market]; **Mande will sollohaul neither bango nor tatcho**: I swear now neither falsely or truly; **holtà**: perimeter; **oopràlyavinate**: sunrise; **rakyàsapatyàv**: night-belief; **bezèti**: dream (n); **chachoonò**: means both righteous (adj) and real (adj); **cshib**: tongue (n); **chachès**: truth (n); **Gajo**: non-Romani; **bridvà**: picked (adj); **rokker**: to speak, usually meaning to speak Romani (v)

salchinyalò: branchy; **tsikooroo zhookels**: puppies; **harèef**: ice; **bootòoshi**: boots; **stràha**: wall; **tahtùy**: cup; **matòo**: hard drink, liquor; **kibir kurla?**: what's the price?; **hoolanò**: master; **tsirkajìs**: clown; **tsìrka**: circus; **agor**: at the end; **choochoonya, rayà**: twigs for basket weaving; **jèpa**: pocket; **hatalì**: money; **polokès**: slowly; **kurpìzavà my kaltsa**: to mend my trousers; **dooymooyalò**: double dealer; **dyàslis iphoo**: thrown to the ground, KO'ed [wrestler's term: 'give him the ground']; **sovavnò**: sleepy (adj); **bùlnoozyava**: talk in one's sleep (v); **lamàda**: a flat stone; **rarorò**: dumb; **razprèyzila**: tale; **ahmàtsi manoosh**: a foolish man; **rokker**: talk in Romani; **gerdèy**: gutter; **hòratiba**: speaking (n): **romanipè**: Roma legend, tradition; **delpesgodì**: to remember

koonjoopàte: in a tangle (adv); **retchka**: duck (n); **retchko**: drake (n); **ràrtigìllichal**: nightingale; **rùkkersamèngri**: squirrel; **kackaràtchi**: magpie; **kàulochìrilo**: blackbird; **weshjook**: fox (n); **wiffler**: pigeon; **bìttikànni**: partridge; **bàrripòari**: peacock; **sèsi**: a voice; **eef**: snow (n); **erikin**: plum (n); **oopràlyavinate**: sunrise; **fòros**: city; **màstooroos**: mystery, as in the mastery of craft, but also craftiness; **lèshi**: corpses; **shoodrò**: cold (adj)

sabàlen: morning, at daybreak; **len**: river; **yakh**: eye (n); **panyalò**: water (n); **bryàgoos**: riverbank; **randlò**: shaved clean (adj); **surnà**: deer; **kookoochin**: snowdrop; **evènd**: winter (n); **pàhni**: frost (n); **erlìdes**: Gypsies living a settled life; **parusyoov**: slush; **garavdò**: hidden (adj); **sàstra**: iron; **akanootnò**: the present, the contemporary (n); **paloonò**: the back one, the one behind; **rarorikanès**: mimic and mimicking

II

1905

I dream backwards half my life. The same snowdrops by the river.
I watch her pick a penèrka of flowers before I speak with her.

She will sell these in the city. I tend ten shire-foals, they
with their full maws of shootlyahà, much prone to bengipè,

nibble the air near her, nudging, nosing at the bouquet.
I play host to them, name by name: their mothers and honours,

the pitav of the eldest, tetìki of the tiniest, how any head of theirs
would outpace an ox at the ploughing, izprevarizehìs mìlya!

but their turf will be tougher, to trot behind the talìga,
strung only when they stray, one day to bear the bandrooki,

from follower to followed, bold brasses on their chokàt.
Next time I would boast less. I am at the river next avìn.

We are young; she is twin to both tribes, the city's, the Roma's.
Our early days are bay and roan, the horse-colours of hours

rising into their running-powers. By midsummer I ask her,
win her father's word, my indais kaìli. Our honeymoon

a honeysuckle hooped over a tsàra, an honour-guard of brood-mares.
We wind through the wide land keeping with the blacksmiths,

firing up forges in each gav, shoeing, prising hoof-rot
from a thousand sprinters, pacers and padders. We eavesdrop

word of wars, red guards in sharp cities, but heed to our horsecraft:
foals topple in their birth-ropes, snickering, half-standing;

horses spring from the smiths' grasp as if raring for the racing.
Our camp shimmers with anvils. Hooves flicker on our outfields.

Reed-birds whose whole lives are spent invisible in rushes,
rigging nests where they will, weaving their worlds from the rayà –

crakes, rails, brown bitterns, whose nests are centres of their earth;
their thin calls correct the spin of the doonyàs: the reed's axis teeters:

everything is in balance. Lift the levels of their lakes, let loose faster foxes
those whole worlds unravel. Rumours ring us; there are red guards

in cities, grey garrisons on the grasslands, and a drought of metal.
We wait on the edges, cry to each other in codes, move only on margins,

unweave our wagon-camps from their usual tsarunò.
Some damn us as daranòok. My young wife sees further.

My beloved spake to me, rise up, my fair one, and come away.
She is white-faced at the kings, a looloodì among thorns.

She takes horse to her city for the feast day of her father
for the evènd is past, the panì is over and gone.

I track her tooryalìste, my horse hammering her hurt grass,
hurt halving me, tearing me, hurling helve after hatchet,

but I cannot catch her. I catch horizons but not her.
Then her city curves into sight; my horse swerves at its river.

Smoke climbs sky-high; flames chew through the rafters.
Red guards race through the roadways, rodav, ratvalilò.

My beloved lies in the reedbeds. The earth melts beneath me
revealing the garavdò, the veiled and unsmelted. Remember.

She is nested in death. I now curse the one who killed her.
Until the day break and the shadows flee away, I balance her body in my arms.

My akooshìba: you will meet me in your mirror: you will remember me.
You, who hold the harness of the officers, remember me.

You, who hone their swords on the whetstone, remember me.
You, who swab the shields of the red guard, remember me.

Who rim the rearing wall, rain arrows over our camps, remember me.
You, who cheat our chililgìrs: cavalry, you will remember me.

Who count the cold coin in the keep, remember me.
You, who bait with barvaypì, from a distance, remember me.

Who wall in our wide fields, which slay us so casually, remember me.
Who slew my beloved, slid her to the waters, remember me.

Remember: we are all one: all who are with us are ourselves.
Our word gallops like grass-fires. You will wither by this word.

I will crash through your kingdoms, calling your kanilipè
to the realms of all Roma. I am riding revenge to you,

to the lip and leap of a distant devlèskere pògya.
O dooymooyalò, judge me, but you will remember me.

Hold the halter of patsyàva. I am riding this curse on you.
I wage war with these words, on your raklò and raklì.

Remember I rank you, as shtòopos, as sapnì.
You are ratvalyaràv, randimè. You rise only to be reaped.

Your names now are nangò, your newborn cshoongadimè.
Cshavàlen who chastised us, we who are chindi-chibengoro.

You will remember me. You will meet me in your mirror,
for I am the asking and answering owlcalls of an akooshìba.

La parhoodìlis. Nettle-dew douses the swords of the nettle,
its microscopic thorns are uplifted and sheathed

in incepts of chlorophyll and unwounding serum.
Boorgoodjìdes smash the nettles, simmer funeral zoomì.

So much for weapons. Tsikìnda in the burial yard,
tsikìnda in my buried heart, we bury her by the river;

burn all her belongings, even our bed. I am barèstar.
I opened to my beloved, but my beloved has withdrawn herself.

Even as she lies there, the light thaw quickens. What hard saying?
Fallow luck sees furthest. A heart trammelled or rammed

on its anvil bleeds visions. Get lost. Get lost, Boorgoodjìdes.
Ride your mares shoeless. Misplace your atlases.

I am your seer. The herald. Again, the one left behind.
I am not your tame dreamer. I have a horse and a whip.

I have a horse and a whip. I could kill you and go.
I ride by the river, nasvalòo of kamav, kalò with meribè,

tether my horse, and stride straight into the fòros
in the òolitsa, and in the boohlò putèka I seek her,

my ozì piryamlòo. I seek her, amà I do not find her.
But the red soldiers that stand guard on the fòros find me,

they smite me, wound me; for the red guards of the stràha
had taken her veil, her life, from her. What is thy beloved

more than another beloved, o thou fairest among women?
What is thy beloved more than another beloved that thou dost so charge us?

penèrka: basket (n); shootlyahà: sorrel (n); bengipè: tricks, quirks (n); pitav: honesty (n); tetìki: nervousness; izprevarizehìs: outrun (v); mìlya: a thousand; talìga: cart, wagon; bandrooki: yoke (n); chokàt: forehead; avìn: dawn, morning; indais: tribe; kaìli: agreement; tsàra: covered wagon; gav: village

rayà: twigs for basket weaving; doonyàs: world; tsarunò: literally 'Gypsy-camp style'; daranòok: cowardly; looloodì: flower (n); evènd: winter (n); panì: rain (n); tooryalìste: circling movement or manoeuvre; helve: the handle of an axe, chisel, hammer [OE]; hurling helve after hatchet: to throw helve after hatchet [OE]: 'to risk everything'; rodav: seeking, hunting; ratvalilò: bloody (adj); garavdò: hidden (adj)

akooshìba: curse (n); chililgìrs: farriers; barvaypì: riches; kanilipè: evil-doing; devlèskere pògya: horizon; dooymooyalò: hypocrite, double-dealer; patsyàva: belief (n); raklò: non-Gypsy boy; raklì: non-Gypsy girl; shtòopos: rubbish, garbage; sapnì: snake; ratvalyaràv: covered with blood (adj); randimè: reaped (adj); nangò: naked (adj); cshoongadimè: bespattered (adj); Cshavàlen: O You People! (voc); chindi-chibengoro: without a tongue

la: her; parhoodìlis: burial [performed swiftly after death; because death is perceived as unclean, everything belonging to a dead Romani is burnt, including their caravan or tent]; Boorgoodjìdes: the blacksmiths' tribe; zoomì: soup; tsikìnda: nettles (n); barèstar: become stone, made of stone; nasvalòo: sick (v); kamav: love (n); kalò: dark (adj); meribè: death (n); fòros: city; òolitsa: streets; boohlò: broad (adj); putèka: paths; ozì: soul (n); piryamlòo: lover; amà: but; stràha: wall (n)

III

1933

A garden inclosed is my spouse; a spring shut up, a fountain sealed.
Awake, north wind; and come, thou south; blow upon my garden.

I sleep but my heart waketh. I dream forwards half my life.
Seven shire horses wade, their tails whish ice-shell. Last lilày on this len

we swam a hundred horses, washing the beasts before we bartered them.
How they tantrummed, the stallions and mares, how their manes sprayed

spectra, halo and rainbow. There is something ahead now,
false water at distance. I have always been asleep. How can I wake now?

I have washed my feet   shall I defile them? I have put off my coat;
how shall I put it on? I rouse again, waking from my last loshalì.

I have been stretched all day in the snow. Sunset stings my eyes.
Flags are flung down, washing poles withdrawn into the eyes of arrow-slits.

Grim gates seal themselves andràl. The drawbridge drags itself up.
Black locks catch on high latches. The city is an anemone, as if a

falling oochipè had run its fingers over its skin. My horses sleep standing.
I feed our hounds on their tying posts. Steppes unravel about me,

the reedbeds shiver with bahtali, with the timid, with garavdò ròmanichìrrilos.
Our camp is empty. They are gone before me. Who will walk out of this wilderness?

I beg of you believe in the Kings, the blacksmiths' tribe, the Boorgoodjìdes
made up of the tamar, true twisters of sàstra, sras or srastrakàni,

who jam the dandalò srast in the jaws, the chamàhoolya, of their kerpèdy,
and ply it, plume it polokès then plakomè rotating the bright akanootnò.

They are gone. Now, seek north wind; and go, thou south; find my people.
A world inclosed is my dream; a spring shut up, and a fountain sealed.

There is always a drab door to a dookhanì, where plague-carriers
are carried and left alive like a second stràha; always the light lock, or

a skylight smiling open; a little wicked wicker gate, a dooymooyalò on duty,
dead to the doonyàs. There is always a way. I slide into the city

sidelong. Sometimes when I am dreaming, when my kings are khizim,
I dream that I am dreaming and, when waking, dream I am waking.

The city dreams it is dozing, its gullible walls propped on each other;
gutters snoring with water. But something is moving: I run seeking:

I the north wind and south, I am come into this fòros.
A boohaloos arcs along the boohlò putèka, a parnò dìkhiba;

moon clouds release shadow, shadow-dancers, their fallen purlèntas.
I slide through the city, sigyarindòs, so sigòo I reach its bare edges,

where nobody sleeps, where nobody lives, where canals in their locks
climb up from the stone-fords, and bright sewage sleeps.

A ràrtigìllichal calls. I reply with wood-speech.
A weshjook barks. I reply with wood-speech.

The boohaloos rotates its white wings and then plunges.
A small cry goes up. The reed's axis teeters.

My kings lie about me. My queens lie about me. They are piled about me.
Shoodrò, they are limb–slight. They have been hiding here all day from me.

Why was I late, who am never late; why am I behind who must herald them.
Their heads are as the most fine gold, their locks black as a raven's.

They are beautiful. They are terrible as an army with banners.
I see the faces of children. I crawl to a willow. I want to touch the one thing that
                                                is alive.

I wake under the tree. Stars wake above my eyelids as white looladì.
I guide my eye's hand to reach one down, one devletlùki lokò.

The wind plucks at the willow: *there are many voices in me.*
I pick belief, apatyàv. It sings in my palm. It asks only that I follow.

What it says, apatyàv, is that my kings have gone before me.
Sorì simensar sì mèn. I can now go on behind them.

I lie beneath this tree, barely breathing, my body taking root,
my hands wrist-deep in leaves. My spine spindles out

nerves to nettle-root and ragwort-root; they utter to each other.
The skull's crown sinks back as if it were shrugging, or forgetting,

and bright hair clings.   – Sèviba.   There is thunder.
One raindrop splatters a patrin, o kolè dyoonaste. The choolì's

rain-sisters join in, suicidally, spraying the vùrba with panì on panì
until the willow seems to writhe and whirl, a vertical vurtsimipuy.

I sense her above me, spooling me sastò into del, still dreaming:
Ì am circling you. In the court of the hayfields I am circling you.

You courted me in the lee of hedgerows, running on the field-side,
oomalyàkom, I keeping to the drom: you invisible, audible,

a flume of finches blowing through the thornfields at my riding.
Sov, she says, *drown in me, drawn up on my shelò of shookaripè.*

Address your armagànos to the àngelas, asanòo mànoosh. I am sky-drowned,
her white throat calling —— *Te Avel Angle Tute Te Avel Angle Tute Te Avel*
Angle Tute

so like a birdcall, the redpoll's, my lòlochìrillo, my new wife singing,
and then she is before me, my wife is before me, my love has come for me.

lilày: summer (n); len: river; loshalì: happiness; andràl: from the inside; oochipè: shadow (n); bahtali: white magic; garavdò: hidden; ròmanichìrrilos: water wagtails; Boorgoodjìdes: the blacksmiths' tribe; tamar: ironsmiths; sàstra, sras, srastrakàni: iron (n); dandalò: jagged; srast: iron (n); chamàhoolya: jaws (n, pl); kerpèdy: pliers; polokès: slow (adv); plakomè: squashed, pressed (adj); akanootnò; the present, the contemporary

dookhanì: hospital; stràha: wall, a defence wall; dooymooyalò: double-dealer; doonyàs: world; khizim: gathered; fòros: city; boohaloos: an owl; boohlò: broad; putèka: paths; parnò: white; dìkhiba: visitation; purlèntas: silk headkerchief; sigyarindòs: hurriedly; sigòo: fast; ràrtigìllichal: nightingale; weshjook: fox; shoodrò: cold

looladì: flowers (n); devletlùki: heavenly (adj); lokò: light (n); apatyàv: belief; Sorì simensar sì mèn: We are all one, all who are with us are ourselves [Romani saying]; sèviba: thunder (n); patrin: leaf, also a page, or a marker left by Roma to tell others of their passing (n); o kolè dyoonaste: beyond, in the other world; choolì: drop (n); vùrba: willow (n); panì: rain (n); vurtsimipuy: a whirlpool; sastò: whole; del: sky, God, heaven (n); oomalyàkom: field; drom: road; sov: sleep (imp: Sleep!): shelò: rope; shookaripè: beauty; armagànos: gift; àngelas: angels; asanòo mànoosh: smiling man; te avel angle tute: may this be before you; lòlochìrillo: redpoll

Whitethroat

Whitesmiths work the tinct tin into leaves.
They could weave, if they chose, a whole whitten of it.

It would glitter, that false wayfarer's tree,
as the whitethorn, or the whitethroat calling from its false leaves.

Dotterel

Through the mists
        above the marsh
                the linked, frantic gestures –

Flight-horizons
        of dotterel –
                shiver into one harmonic bridge.

This shore arcs in
        inventing itself over
                a reflux of wings, freshets, light.

Architecture of air
        running in the wake
                of a beak's sift,

Precisions escaping
        before it: edges,
                chases, bevels.

Through the mists
        above the marsh,
                the linked, frantic gestures –

Dotterel swirl,
        hail blown
                above marsh light.

Redpoll

As if she had spilt
from cherries, from holly, from
a shake of nightshade.

Goldcrests

'Cedar-cedar-cedar-cedar-sissu-see' – song of a goldcrest

She sings light, he sings lightly, from the pine-needled nestcup.
He shifts lightly; she shifts light, among the burrs in the nestcup.
How slightly, how very slight, the sky shrinks to their eggshell hue.
How slight, how very slightly, light wakes from their eggshell hue.
He sees lightly, she sees light, in the pine-needle dark.
She sang light, he sang lightly, among the cedars in the dark.

Red-Throated Pipit

Pincering to nests
   On heathbell or heather,
Fetched like rain
   Above fjeld, fjord,

Rained down like flume
   Blown back up the big fall,
Imping in the sedge
   Of skreebeds, a joskin.

Onset of iceblink,
   Lumber of ice-foot,
Fleered across Europe,
   Flat to Sahara,

Flinching under cloudbank
   To dank fiumara
Chipped in its ear, his
   Flint *chup!* and *skee-az.*

Siskin

                                                 on birch and alder

                           cast between catkins

      Kin to the whisper

Goldfinches

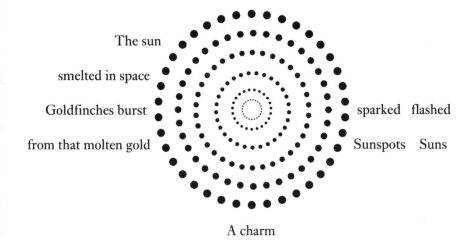

The sun

smelted in space

Goldfinches burst   sparked   flashed

from that molten gold   Sunspots   Suns

A charm

Snowfinches

for M.S. at sixty

The musicians are late, delayed by snowdrifts, but nobody minds.
Snowfinches are roosting in the hall's roof. Our warmth woke them.
The hearth uplights their underwings. They flicker between rafters.
Carols or carillons. Carillons or carols. What shall we hear from our artists?

To Feed the Dead Who Would Come Disguised as Birds

There were examples,
too many, the small people said. See, they
called, how things turn on each other
and a sleeping sickness leaks through
our language, how our Gypsy symbols spelled
no clear counsel.

Example: a ride
by the river was a death wish; a flit
in the woods might end in a fight.
So what of the nightjar you were
seeking. It was the wrong time to listen,
that night hunting it.

Look, learn, sweet watcher.
There was ground to be prized in pitching here,
those small people said. The Sídhe held
we had choices: the fish in this
river or the hares in those woods. *Those* woods,
through their white feathers,

are dark spruce. Christmas
pines, snow, one starved, occasional redbreast.
Take their bird's disguise, traveller.
They have learnt thin paths to show you
their hidden way. It was strong of you to
stride out with your heart

bare, seeking counsel.
How could they counsel, they, the watching dead –
graft to you their will of stillness
when you were snared by that river,
those woods, by Red Guards returning to their
village for Christmas.

Sídhe: (Gaelic) ancestors, spirits of nature, goddesses and gods

Bears

for Gabriel John Keenan Morley

PawPaw and Paprika, two great bears of the Egyptians
of Lancashire, the Witches' County, Chohawniskey Tem

who, when our camp plucked its tents and pulled out its maps,
walked steadily with the wagons, ambling, always ambling,

all across the open pages of wet England, footing
as far as Pappin-eskey Tem, the flat Duck County,

crossing to Curo-mengreskey Gav, the Boxers' Town;
padded on to Paub-pawnugo Tem, Apple-Water County

as good for bears as for their Gypsy masters, although
who is master is moot after much apple-water;

then to bide by Bokra-mengreskey Tem, Shepherds' County,
for their collies are trained not to bark at bears, but slyly, gently,

slink big-eyed as children behind their shepherd's greeting.

Ambling, bears, always ambling... mooching to Mi-develeskey Tem,
My God's Town, the God for all bears too,

God of paws and padding, of Polar, Kodiak and Koala;
sniffing superiorly through Dinelo Tem, the Fools' County;

circling with our circus to Shammin-engreskey Gav, Chairmakers' Town,
nosing north through Lil-engreskey Gav, a Town Made of Readers,

then paws over eyes for Kaulo Gav, the Black Town;
joy at Jinney-mengreskey Gav, the Sharpers' Town;

to Lancashire as it was then, wider county of white witches,
to the clean camps, to the great brown bears of the Egyptians.

To PawPaw and Paprika, backwards in time they go, pad pad. *Goodbye*.

The bears' route: Lancashire to Lincolnshire to Nottingham to Herefordshire to Sussex
to Canterbury *through* Suffolk to Windsor through Oxford to Birmingham to Manchester
and Lancashire.

A Boy Casting Snow on Winter Barley

a variation of Paul Celan

The months are hairs combed over each other, or crushed
papers in a cellar. December is growing, fur on my lip.

December's the hair on a monk's fingers, a book pulled open,
a boy throwing snow at the first winter crops. Your hair is twisted up;

it is dark and it makes me imagine shells or cloud-shells, a boat
nudging into a rainy lake. A boat, a book pulled open or over,

fear, a shrew squirming in my fingers... December's black hook.
December's lake water. Can I sing? Can I live through this winter?

A small lyric on my palm. I stand on the shore of a lake.
As far as a boat may be rowed, the colour of aspens

colourless by night as I grow in shade and my age deepens.
I speak of loving you as I speak to you about hands,

shells or clouds. I push the boats with my fingers and they nod
in our bloodstreams, lovers crushed together, or clouds

heaped in a downpour. Walking from the forest I find myself
necklaced with bared hands. December is gaining on me.

A Static Ballroom

She has squeezed a pipette, a teat, a trigger,
has pinched the heart, its very life out, she

presses her eye to the lens of a microscope,
the muzzle of it, the sawn-off cylinder of it

but no one will request an explanation.

Her sight stamps the earth where she has buried herself.
Her vision rushes through its lenses; and she

runs through those galleries, bursting the door
where she finds them, it, a static ballroom – of dancers

as they were when a bomb exploded.

Nobody requests an explanation. They are closing
their mouths, the only mass moving; closing

their lives, they can say nothing. She arcs
across the glass floor of the scarlet ballroom

in a micrograph of her own blood plasma;

strides through herself, her eye dancing.
The first time she knows herself this thoroughly.

The last time she will be in such company.
Gazing at the slide of her arctic reflection

in the hall of her blood, the orchestra silent.

Garèzi Gilì

Don't get up, don't answer the phone;
there's a place for everything and you are alone.
This place hasn't even got a name.
(It's where you go when you're ashamed.
You know by now you're the one to blame.)
Don't take on, or tread your luck,
don't tempt the terrors behind your back.
This place is trying, and you are tried.
(Now you know your face has died,
its muscles have locked along your lies.)
This space is you. It speaks your number.
It's where you dump your clothes by the river
and pull out towards the deeper water.
(Where you'll gain nothing by plunging under
except the skill, don't answer it, to remember.)

garèzi: vengeance; **gilì**: song

An Ice Queen

We, you, I – in our mirror she finds an error
nothing so trite as a crack or cross: its mass
of metals slips with her gravity's lunge, where we
are pulled into the lulls of her corners, then cornered.
The great house passes for what we expect. Expected,
we take the valet's low door and the concealed corridor.
What are her high demands but answers to our answers?
We tread shells to the shores of her hard rooms.
A servant shifts in us, a craving; we long to serve,
lounging in the cellar's dark matter, for any mark
of notice, any flickering of those fingers. Her rings
we have learned to kneel to, where our slit lips move.
She was clever and she was ice-clear, those near
the light of her work left off their own work
to tend hers, feed her starveling grate. How late
she recognised their shades, who served, who paid.
Her appetite for the svelte pear, for sex, for lied prayer
knowing nothing comes to nothing, so that feeding on
mouthing right things grants her more years, no more
than is worth anyone's while, except her snow-child's.
Three, two, one. Those fascinated by her gravity, try
counting back to when you became so : so the same
vanity trips us, traps us in our error. She is that mirror
we grow hard enough to gaze into. Then melt through.

Nets at Gennesaret

for Peter Scupham

One mirror: he walked the water
   and the water
allowed it: a web's face of surface tensions:
a pond–skater's halo. *We have toiled all night*
   and have taken
   nothing: nevertheless, at thy word.

'I sank three nets in the lake's edge,
   each with a plumb,
lattice corks strung skew-whiff of the ante-lines,
mesh thinned to catch swimming needles of elver.'
   And when this was done
'the taut sea exploded with fish'.

Sky High Ice

for Vicki Ann Behm

My friends
Say I have a light touch on
A tall ladder. Those winters kicking
Up frozen water in sheer streambeds in high country.
This is the same art, no?

I made
The ascent to the apex
Of their library, teetering like
A gyroscope, the ladder slung like a drunken mast
To four worn climbing ropes.

For what
Art? A witch ball, to string up
With fish-line to the uppermost reach,
Fractious as a twirled globe, that fat mirror swallowing
The room's slews, tilts and true;

Below:
Two friends, the kind, taut ropes,
The ladder itself, double-crossing
Me, that Janus ball mirroring its Jacob's ladder
Above my frantic hand:

Air's rung
On which to grasp, then to tread
More skilfully than on sky high ice:
Its mantraps and undermines, its sloped heavens running
With copper melt-water.

The Ideal

The sun, gradually
going blind behind cypresses, pines, lowers
  a red crown at the sea's surface
and leaves it lolling on the clouds' banners
  the while it takes to see

  this physics of light–
scattering; how wavelengths are also fronts, war,
  skied defeats, as though high kingdoms
made out of sheer light went down clashing for
  an ideal of night.

European Larch

Collins Field Guide to British and European Trees

The Alps –
    replaced by Norway Spruce
        in colder, wetter areas –
            with ranges
            in the Tatra and Sudetan
    plains and mountains of Poland.
        Long cultivated and abundant:
            in older plantations, shelterbeds
            and parks,
away from cities and the driest, drabbest areas.

Timber
    tough and rot-resistant;
        Tatra and Sudetan forms make
            the finest
            variety plantation trees.
    Variants: 'Pendula', that
        broad and depressed-looking tree displays
            exaggeratedly weeping shoots;
            most rare;
even rarer, spectacularly *weeping* cultivars.

Shape: spire-
    like, on a trunk straight up
        only in the finest, sheltered
            trees; often
            broad and characterful in age
    in arid or exposed sites.
        The fine shoots *hang* under the branches.
            Blond in winter. More finely, spiki-
            ly twig-
gy – set against, say, the Ginkgo or, say, a Swamp Cypress.

Saplings
grow wildly twisting trunks.
They *un*bend with maturity.
Leaves: vivid
green, two pale bands beneath. Cones:
soon brown: egg-shaped when ripe, their
scales *not or scarcely not curving*.
Female flowers: bright as rubies in
mid-spring
among new green needles. They are easily overlooked.

Sycamore

Alpine,
spire-like   in her timber   scaffolds
she has   been climbing   the firm rungs   of   summer,
prying   for untried   holds in   that chimney
of air,   pushing   aside   old leaves
as if   they   were bad   luck.
It   should   have been a   good
season,   all the equipment   new
and shining;   green guarantees   of
dawns and   rapid nights.   With
each move she   claims
some   slight   expanse.
Upturned   to a false
horizon,   she can
pause,   gaze
on the falling
distance, find
rooting, rigging.
The rigging of
a sycamore
is capsized
into winter.
Her limbs
stiffen, then
her used
dressings
fall where
they will,
hand-held,
palm up,
skeletal.
Hearing,
hearing   the red avalanche   scarlet   leaves.
without climbing   this far.   Those splashed
She,   standing   clear.

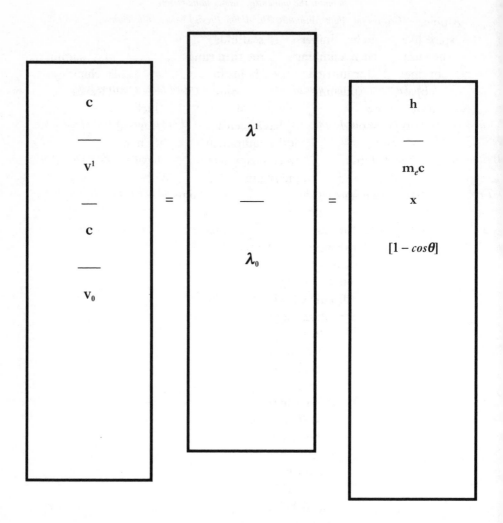

$$\frac{\dfrac{c}{v^1}}{\dfrac{c}{v_0}} = \frac{\lambda^1}{\lambda_0} = \frac{h}{m_e c} \text{ x } [1 - cos\theta]$$

Texts to the Inventor of Italics

'to mimic the humanists' cursive handwriting'
Created for Aldus Manutius, The Aldine Press, Venice: 16th century

The human face, the curse of type   *A cursed face, a writing type*

Cursives written on the face and hand   *Face to face, a type of cursing*

Writing humans   Face it, type   *Face it, human   Face the mimic*

To mimic their type: to new their face   *Hand to hand, writing human*

A type of face   *A type of hand*

Aldine   *and Alpine*

A type of cursive humanism

A Printer's Rose

for Tony Ward

SING: the hew the heft of the St Albans Rose of the Pierre Chandelier
Of Aldus Pius Manutius & of Ehard Oglin we sing
We sing of the Aldine Dolphin twined about its anchor
Of glyph consistent serif of circumflex & stuttering
Of Aldus Pius Manutius & of Ehard Oglin we sing
Of Fust and Schoeffer non-breaking space of read-error of Caxton
Of glyph consistent serif of circumflex & stuttering
Of anchoring mark anchorite caesura & High Treason
Of Fust and Schoeffer non-breaking space of read-error of Caxton
Of Geneva & of Grub St of Denventer & of Venice
Of anchoring mark anchorite caesura & High Treason
Of hot metal & slush pile of purple prose of promise
Of Geneva & of Grub St of Denventer & of Venice
Of Chapman's darg o' Embro or Columbies de Toulouse
Of hot metal & slush pile of purposed prose of 'polish'
& finishing strokes & colophons & ampersands & typos
Of Chapman's darg o' Embro   of Columbies de Toulouse
Of the hew the heft of the St Albans Rose & the Pierre Chandelier
Of finishing strokes   colophons   ampersands typos
Sing over   of ten dolphins   twined about   this anchor

Architects of the Frari, Venice

What of our hands? With them we request, summon, dismiss… keep silent and what not else,
rivalling the tongue.

We sail fifty crossbeams over such seas of air.
We muscle stones upon their brothers to meet them half-way.
We stand their ground, if ground is to be had on a bed of sea,
on which everything – our calculation, our conjecture – is a kiss on clay.
Finished, we have no choice but to go, to grow obtuse, at sea,
return in darker worlds, to render up with stone tongues
our rage: Antonio Canova's heart in his isocelean tomb.
A fig in a box. His right hand sawn loose for the Accademia…

Of separating body from form, shore from shore:
our hands held the white tides… Now tides lap us on our shelf.
Canova's hand now? Applauding itself against itself?
We raised masts upon the sea. We roofed that ship of stone.
We held one straightening plumb-line,
trusted its true to the paths of the sea. We sailed such air.

Croix Pantoum : Tenth Christmas for Isaac

A schoolyard under snow's a solid rink in secret.
Nobody wants to understand this, except the caretaker.
He crosses the space, a green man, spading slush to the edges.
Salt's scattered. Dip your boots. The yard's porridge.
Nobody wants to understand this, except the caretaker.

The sun does its work, scanning it like a photocopier.
Salt's scattered. Dip your boots. The yard's porridge.
The sun takes the yard, dissolves it, recasts it as cloud-forms
and sun does its work, scanning them, a photocopier
Clouds flock together. Trembling, they look down with long faces

Now take the yard, dissolve it, recast it as cloud-forms.
Let fog freeze on a wing-mirror. On the mirror of a robin's wing
Clouds flock together, trembling. They look down with long faces
as the teachers' cars cough slowly, old women in libraries
and fog freezes on wing-mirrors, on the mirrors of a robin's wings.

Once the bell yells, it's chaos, the kids skidding like car-crashes;
the teachers' cars cough clouds, old men leaving libraries.
He crosses space — the green man — spading slush to its edges.
Once the bell yells, it's chaos, the kids skid like car-crashes.
The schoolyard under snow's a solid rink. His secret.

The Waves

My child grows beyond
his tipped turrets of sodden sand.

He recreates pure
impatient forms from seawater.

The castles dry in no time;
he, unaware of the lifting foam.

As water strikes his world's edges
it overwhelms small villages.

As language is tsunami.
It carves half-worlds we

live and die in. There this
comparison dries.

Language became a wave, a break,
an intricate flat world in its wake.

It is flown and broken.
It is made and unmade of our children.

Ludus Coventriae

for Isaac

These were marginal people I had met only rarely
And the end of the whole household meant that no grief was seen;
Never have people seemed so absent from their own deaths.

Introduction

This poem tells the story of the city of Coventry's destruction in World War
II. Coventry was one of the leading cultural and trading centres in medieval
England. Its Mystery Plays of that time were famed throughout the country:
Shakespeare is believed to have attended a performance. The plays drama-
tise episodes from the Bible and were staged by local trade guilds or
'mysteries'.

The movement 'The Charges on Midsummer Night' uses financial records
of medieval stagecraft for the Mystery Plays in Coventry. There are three
time-frames within the movement 'November the Fourteenth, Nineteen
Forty-One': the morning of 14 November 1941 before the major blitz; the
first few seconds of that bombardment; and medieval Coventry at the time
of the midsummer Mystery Plays.

o

On the nights of the World War II raids, radio beams were transmitted from
two distant points on the coast of Europe, intersecting at 90 degrees over
Coventry, creating an invisible cross in the sky. This was used as a precise
radar target for the Luftwaafe. The German code name for the operation
was 'Moonlight Sonata'.

Fifty-six per cent of the city's houses were damaged or destroyed. The dead
and dying lay piled high in temporary morgues, or under the miles of
burning rubble, as rescue squads tried to pull from the debris those still
alive. Refuges were hit, burying people alive: 'our shelter was like a cage of
frightened animals'.

The Charges on Midsummer Night

- p*ai*d for a pece of tymber for ye Axeltre, & for Nayles for it, ye Pagent whereof halfe is to spare in William Catesby's house
- Item payd for Sope for all ye wheeles
- Item payd for *3* Worlds
- Item payd for payntyng Hell Mouth and me*n*dying hyt
- Item payd for openyng and shuttyng the Dores and kypyng the Wynd

- Item payd for settyng the Worlds on ffyer & blacking ye Sowles facys
- Item payd to the *3* damnyd Sowles & *3* Saved Sowles
- Item payd thus to *2* Demens
- Item payd the *2* wormes of Consyens
- Item p*ai*d to Death

- Item payd to the Mother of Death
- Item payd ffor a peyre of gloves ffor God
- Payd up also for the gybbyt of Jei3e
- Item payd to Mr Fawsto*n* for hangyng Judas
- Item p*ai*de to Mr Fawsto*n* for his Coc-crowyng

- Item payd for *3* Angells
- Item paide ffor wasshyng the Angells surplisses
- Item payd to Iosephe
- Item payd to God
- And also paide to the Spirite of God

- Item payd to Jesus
- Item payd to Mary
- Item payd to Pylate
- Item to the litell dying Chyld
- Item payd for this Prologe

November the Fourteenth, Nineteen Forty-one

Their world, and that of the Catesbys in Cook Street
differed, like
the eggshell hue of the wren and linnet.

○

'Aslepe as Coventree this faire morning'
(the sycamores drip from pressure prior to the eclipse)

whose farms lie smack against canal-basins,
whose long-faced beasts yawn and bask in their midge-clouds.

So, sleep, as Coventry sleeps this morning
with low sky catching alight from streetlamps.
The sweeping bus views from house to town,
Herod the king, in his raging.

○

Rejoice, rejoice, all that here be!
The angel that has brought this child here.
So now let us all prepare
Our temple and sweep the yards.
God's son who hangs upon the tree
Has cleared away our care.

Glossy stare and red squirrel
oblivious in eave or dray
are mass and matter
by close of day.

o

Out of desert, from the hard stone
three air raid wardens run, three kings
late up with pick, spade, lantern,
tracing the star of each explosion and making there.

For most stay put,
squat among their own brick and bone
or worse, stray underground
beneath the burning stairs or buried cellar.

o

Behold it has come to pass
That Christ, our just Messiah
Is bought and sold by Judas.
To pacify his father's wrath
He became a man, he ransom pays for man
As he hangs there nailed to the sky. O Lord,
As thou hath bought our hearts
And suffered on high Calvary,
Recomfort us, both slow and spry,
That in thy truth we live and die.

Out of danger shall us release.
Out of whose dangers?
The sword or sharpened cross?

It is the bombers' cross-wires
radio-signallers
that drag those planes across.

He is come to set the world on fire.
Red, the town is fallen; alight,
a light; and all its temples fired.

○

With low sky catching alight from streetlamps,
enough light to register from one thousand feet above
nettle-tree architecture of church and spire –
its foreshortened spear, gimlet-eyed cockerel –
sufficient to land on almost, for a horsefly
or a linnet, or firebombs too.

The spire writhes in high pressure prior to the eclipse.
Fire-rods brim the blackening moon-circle.

Billy forgets. *This is not the morning after,*
it is the morning before.

Godiva pouts in state from his locker-door.

○

With low sky catching alight from streetlamps
there Billy is, workshying, dribbling a football to the shopfloor.

Inside, the cleaners sluice the floors of its blue dye.

In the yard, rain rinses – 'that's where the foreman Dan
chucked up' – clots of human flesh, eel-flesh, peas, fried potato.

o

Billy, head-down like a hod of stones after long carrying:
gently and gentled into balance on his pillow; and the day
unloaded stone by stone as though ready for slow walling;
is when he feels the tilt, and the grip goes sliding.

Cows clop and gawk
in a blacked-out stall.
Midges struggle, go still
in spider nets on streetlamps.

Sycamores drip. Coventry sleeps.
Sirens wake. Farmers
stare up at stars
moving over their fields into the city.

o

The canal surface shivers
with each detonation.
A bus cuts its lights.
Factories wail. Billy remembers.

His feet slide on his blood.
The Lord is our shelter.
He has come to.
He has come to set the world on fire.

Moleskin gloves and polypropylene;　　○　　head of a mallard;

pashed dishevelled nest;　　○　　cloudburst of milestones;

of frosted manure;

○

of buckram coaches flouncing up from the exploding museum;

○

pink snow of records (administrative, personal);　　○　　axe of a pub-sign;

arrows,　apparently human bones;　○
flung gravel: horse-teeth or stun-stones;　　○

○

stethoscopes in showers, and syringes;　　○　　splatter of Coventry

Blue dye;　○　cartoon dancing brickwall;
○　razed bowling greens;

strutting graveslabs;　　○　　hail of stained glass;

a child's kaleidoscope: a hatchet;　　○

a bus hovering in house-high air;　　○

its engine bouncing off five walls and still crawling towards Nuneaton.

Park Street ash, and behind that, Pilate
rinsing his mitts as the crowd thins out.
We shall show that as we can

the dog-watch on Trinity and St Michael's
breaking to wash brick-muck from the corpses.

○

For their world, and that of the Catesbys in Cook Street
differed, like
the eggshell hue of the wren and linnet.

'You Were Broken' opens on an image of an araucaria in a poem of the same title by Ungaretti.

'In Cold Dimensions': the epigraph is from 'The Minimal' by Theodore Roethke.

'Sesì o Lety U Písku': the Nazi concentration camp at Lety U Písku was responsible for the eradication of more than half of the Roma population in the Czech lands. The Czech population often supported the extermination, especially members of the Protectorate police force. It is the site, today, of a factory farm for 13,000 pigs.

'Shookàr mooklò chàv': 'The Bonnie Broukit Bairn', 'synthetic Scots' poem in Hugh MacDiarmid's *Sangschaw* (1925): 'Mars is braw in crammasy, / Venus in a green silk goun, / The auld mune shak's her gowden feathers, / Their starry talk's a wheen o' blethers, / Nane for thee a thochtie sparin', / Earth, thou bonnie broukit bairn! / – But greet, an' in your tears ye'll drown / The haill clamjamfrie! [*broukit*: neglected; *bairn*: child; *braw*: handsome; *crammasy*: crimson; *wheen o' blethers*: pack of nonsense; *greet*: weep; *clamjamfrie*: collection].

'Songs of Songs': from the Song of Solomon. Traces of King James English are kicked over; some trail is left.

'Kings': the *Book of the Wisdom of the Egyptians* deals in field-knowledge of the Romani. It is a kind of hedgerow school book for travelling people. It contains sayings for survival, for living on edges, including within the margins of error imposed by the demands and prejudices of Gajo (non-Gypsies) should offence be taken, and the law, or worse, be thrown against a travelling group or tribe. It is also a moral and practical guide. For example, on manners: 'The man who has not the whip-hand of his tongue and his temper is not fit to go into company'. On patríns or Gypsy way-markers: 'We flings handfuls of grass down at the head of the road we takes, or we makes with the finger a cross-mark on the ground, or we sticks up branches of trees by the side of the hedge.' The epigraph to 'Kings':

Cav acoi, pralor, pen, se the nav of a lil, the sherro-kairipen of a pura kladjis
of the Roumany tem: the Borobeshemescrotan or the lav-chigaripen between
ye jinneynengro ta yi sweti; or the merri-penskie rokrapen
chiv'd by the zi oprey the truo.

from the *Lil of Romano Jinnypen*

78

My language sources for this poem include the website on Romani culture, the Patrin Web Journal (www.geocities.com/~patrin) and its Romanichal Word List. I have also used *The Gypsy–English/English–Gypsy Concise Dictionary* by Atanas Slavov (New York: 1999). Two phrases, including the epigraph to 'Kings', are adapted from *Romano Lavo-Lil* by George Burrow, 1974 edition. The phrase, 'little wicked wicket gate', comes from Edwin Muir's 'The Castle'. Atanas Slavov writes in *The Gypsy–English/English–Gypsy Concise Dictionary*: 'Word stress does not play a significant role in the Gypsy language. It is presented in this work the way words were pronounced by the Gypsies we interviewed. If the interviewees or the written sources we used show differences in applying stresses in certain words, we do not show them'. Stressed vowels are shown as à, è, ì, ò, ù, òo. In this poem, where a single word in Romani has two or more meanings in English, all these meanings should be brought into play: 'for what's righteous in speech, chachoonò, is word-twin for what's real'.

'To Feed the Dead Who Would Come Disguised as Birds' is a line from the poem 'Dedication' by Czesław Miłosz. The Gaelic 'Sídhe' or 'Sìth' referred first to the earth mounds that were thought to be home to a supernatural race related to the fey of other traditions, and later to these inhabitants themselves.

'A Boy Casting Snow on Winter Barley' is a variation on lines and images in Paul Celan's poem 'Talglicht' ('Tallow Lamp').

'Nets at Gennesaret': Matthew 5: 5–6

'Translucent Jiyūshi Banners': read these across for Compton's equation for the physics of light scattering. Read them down for scattered light.

'Texts to the Inventor of Italics' and 'A Printer's Rose': Aldus Manutius adopted the anchor and dolphin as the printer's mark (or rose) for the Aldine Press, in Venice, in the sixteenth century. He also invented italics, 'a new typeface that mimicked the cursive handwriting of humanist writers'.

'Architects of the Frari, Venice': set in the church of that name, built in the fourteenth century. Antonio Canova, the Italian Neoclassical sculptor and painter, was born in Possagno, Treviso, 1757, the son of a stone-cutter. Canova died in Venice, 1822. His heart is entombed in the Frari; his making hand placed in the Accademia; the rest of his body is buried in his birth-town. The epigraph is adapted from Montaigne's essay 'An Apology for Raymond Sebond'.

'Ludus Coventriae': what we know as *Ludus Coventriae* is a collection of Mystery Plays that were once thought to have been presented in Coventry (the plays as such are not *of* Coventry). 'The Coventry Carols', however, are a series of songs from *The Pageant of the Shearmen and Taylors* and *The Pageant of the Weavers*. Members of those guilds and also perhaps professional players performed these 'true' Coventry Corpus Christi plays in Coventry during the celebrations on Corpus Christi Day, the religious festival closest to midsummer. The carols within the plays have entered folk memory as lullabies. 'Ludus Coventriae' borrows phrases from these plays and excerpts from the carols. 'The Charges on Midsummer Night' is freely adapted from *Records of Early English Drama: Coventry*, edited by R.W. Ingram. The epigraph is from 'The Entertainment of War' in *City* by Roy Fisher. A fuller version of this poem is available in chapbook form from Prest Roots Press.